Manifesting Rituals

Manifesting Rituals

POWERFUL DAILY PRACTICES TO MANIFEST YOUR DREAM LIFE

EMMA MUMFORD

greenfinch

Contents

The Messages

Manifestation and Abundance

Spirituality

Money Mindset

Introduction

Welcome to *Manifesting Rituals*. This is your very own sacred manifestation guide, designed to work with your intuition in order to provide you with the tools you need to flourish in all areas of your life. I can't wait for you to dive in and deepen your connection with yourself and your inner wisdom.

If you're new to my work, then welcome. I'm the UK's leading law of attraction expert; the bestselling author of *Positively Wealthy* and *Hurt, Healing, Healed*; host of the number one spirituality podcast on iTunes, *Spiritual Queen's Badass Podcast*; and a YouTuber and speaker.

I first discovered the law of attraction in 2016, when I went through what I call my first 'spiritual awakening' during the lowest point in my mental health journey. Since then, the law of attraction has changed my life and mental health in so many beautiful and abundant ways. I set up my Spiritual Queen brand and business in 2017, and over the years I've shared the

channelled manifestation tips and tools that helped me with
hundreds of thousands of people through my social media
channels and books. It's my mission to help people turn their
dream life into an abundant reality through the power of
manifestation and spirituality.

First, let me explain what the law of attraction is and how you
can use it to achieve your dream life.

The law of attraction is one of the seven energetic laws of
the Universe; it is the belief that we can attract anything we
desire into our lives (whether that involves relationships, career
opportunities, money, love or even feelings and emotions –
there are no limits to what we can attract).

It is all about having a positive and grateful mindset and being
conscious that if we can see something in our mind, we can
hold it in our hands. Like attracts like.

'A bit like karma' is the best way I can explain the law of attraction to you. What you put out into the world, you get back. For example, if you are being loving, kind and happy, you are going to attract lots of incredible miracles into your life, including more love. But if you are being negative, expecting the worst to happen and doubting everything – then guess what? Your life isn't going to feel too positive. Try to see the Universe as a big mirror reflecting your inner world and energy onto your outer experiences.

The law of attraction also teaches us that we are constantly thinking and speaking things into existence – in short, wherever our energy goes, it will manifest into our reality. The Universe matches our energy, which means we attract whatever we are energetically matched to in life. You get to choose what you experience – so choose positivity, abundance and joy!

The Five Steps
of the Law of Attraction

Traditionally, in books and teachings, the law of attraction has three steps: ask, believe, receive. While I feel these steps are absolutely necessary, I found very quickly along my personal manifesting journey that they were not deep or thorough enough. So, when I was writing my first manifestation book, I sat down and considered all that I had learned so far, and I channelled five powerful steps that now feature throughout all my work. Many people tell me how much more sense these steps make and how the law of attraction feels more achievable when following them.

1 Ask The first and most important step in the law of attraction is to ask the Universe/God/Source/Divine – whatever it is you connect with – for what you desire. It is really important to know exactly what you want and to be specific. Don't worry if you have absolutely no idea right now what it is you want in life; the Universe will soon help you out. I always find that focusing on things that bring me joy is a great way to establish what I want. You don't just have to manifest material things. You can manifest emotions, answers and guidance galore! You can even manifest to be shown what your next step should be. The way to ask the Universe can be as simple as saying it out loud – for example, 'Universe, I would like to manifest my monthly salary increasing.' I always like to add the words 'and so it is' at the end, in order to see it as done. You can keep a goals list, write it down as an affirmation, say your manifestation out loud, think it or put it on a vision board. These are all ways of asking, and you only need to ask once.

2 Believe The second step is to believe that your desire will manifest at the perfect time. Some of you may think, 'Well, I just asked – so how come my money, dream career and hunky husband aren't knocking at my door?!' The answer is divine timing. The Universe has a set timeline for you, and everything will manifest at exactly the right time. Enjoy that process, too.

It is no fun if you get everything at once – what would you then focus on manifesting? If you find it hard to believe that your desire can be yours, ask for a sign. Connect to your angels, spirit guides or simply the Universe and ask for a sign that your desire has been heard. Take a look at your inner world to see if there are any limiting beliefs, fears or blocks standing in the way of you and your desire. Explore any blocks that do come up and work to release them. Belief can take some time, so be sure to do daily positive practices and exercises that will help raise your vibration, energy and self-love in order to be in the best possible place to receive your manifestation.

3 Trust This important step is one that I have added to the manifestation process. It may sound similar to 'believe', but the two are quite separate. There will be a period when you are waiting for your manifestation to appear. Manifestation is a co-creation process with the Universe so, in this step, you need to meet the Universe halfway with inspired and aligned action. Essentially, this means acting as if you already have your desire. For example, if you want to manifest your dream partner, you would date yourself, commit to yourself, take inspired action and love yourself. After all, if you had your dream partner you would be relaxed, feeling loved and getting on with your life. You wouldn't be sitting indoors waiting on a text or feeling miserable. So, really connect to the feelings you would have if your heart's desire were here right now, and embody them fully! Think about what action you need to take to put yourself in the field of opportunity with your desire – for example, updating your CV or resume, or planning what outfit to wear for an important event so you can dress to impress.

4 Let go Arguably one of the most important steps in the law of attraction, this is another one that I have added. Although letting go is vital to the manifestation process, for some reason most law of attraction methods skip past it. So, let it all go! It seems confusing that you should ask for your desire and then forget all about it, right? Crazy, I know, but it actually makes things happen so much faster. Letting go means that you are totally okay with either outcome. If you want or need something so badly that you become desperate about it, you risk putting out a vibration of lack, so that's what you will attract more of: lack. Believing your desire will manifest, while at the same time being really grateful for what you have now and accepting the possibility of a different outcome, is an absolute game changer. This is the miracle: seeing how far you have come, honouring your growth and not even needing the manifestation anymore. You still hold that manifestation as your end goal, but you release how and when it will happen. By doing this, you will attract your desire more quickly; and by living in the now, having fun and focusing on other things, you let the Universe get to work!

5 Receive This is the final step: receiving your manifestation. Receiving is still a part of the process, so really challenge yourself to get into the energy of receiving – how much do you allow yourself to receive in all areas of your life? It is a time to celebrate, so let the partying begin! You may receive signs, numbers or even snippets of intuition that your manifestation is on the way. I often sense something the day before it happens. If you do, just relax and let yourself be excited! Honour your journey, thank the Universe and be grateful that your desire has been delivered to you.

Why I Created this Book

After creating my first oracle deck, *Spiritual Queen Oracle Cards*, I felt the pull to create an affirmation oracle book that included deeper meanings and rituals to help you, the reader, deepen your practice with affirmations. I wanted to enable you through the power of ritual to embody the energy of these words and to manifest your desires. There are many affirmation decks and books available, but few of them come with this practical advice. For example, what happens if you don't automatically believe an affirmation? Or what should you do if it doesn't feel good to repeat an affirmation time and time again?

It is because I wanted to answer these questions that I created this manifestation oracle book. I aim to be practical with the law of attraction and I love helping people embody and manifest their desires through tools and practices that work, bringing about huge results in the process. Embodiment is so important with manifestation, and these rituals have all been created to help ground you and bring you into your body so that you can fully embrace the energy of your desires.

So why rituals? Traditionally, rituals have been closely associated with religion and religious ceremonies. According to the official definition, a ritual is a sequence of activities involving gestures, words, actions or revered objects. Rituals were first documented at the earliest stage of religion and the word 'ritual' was first recorded in English in 1570.

Over time, the term 'ritual' has become much more widely used and has been integrated into many spiritual and non-religious practices. Rituals, I believe, are a commitment to yourself and your practice in that moment. Although many well-known manifestation and spiritual rituals are based upon the seasons, essentially, any ritual is a devotion to yourself and the Universe, whether it's a birthday ritual, self-love ritual, abundance ritual or a health ritual.

Rituals allow us to become deeply present and intentional with our time. They also help to cultivate consistency, productivity and momentum with our manifesting practice. Rituals are a deeply personal practice and the great thing is that they can be totally personal to you.

Another way of looking at rituals is as a way to romanticize your life. This is one of my favourite practices, as rituals are absolutely a form of self-love, too. When we ritualize and romanticize the smaller moments in life and our mundane day-to-day habits, we create the opportunity for magic to enter into our life, too.

You can start to romanticize your life by considering this question: what would be a loving thing to do for yourself today? A romanticizing ritual I love to follow during a busy work week is to take time during my lunch break to make a coffee in my fancy coffee machine and eat some of my favourite biscuits while sitting outside in my garden. It may seem simple, but for me this brings the magic of rituals into my day really easily.

Another act of ritualizing your day could be while brushing your teeth. In your mind, you could think about what you're grateful for or even repeat some affirmations in the mirror. Both of these are simple but very practical ways that you can invite the power of rituals into your everyday life.

A common misconception when it comes to rituals is that they take up too much time or that they can't be easily integrated into a busy lifestyle. From my own experience and with numerous clients over the years, I have found that by ritualizing your life you actually create more time for what's important, your priorities and for yourself. As we know, like attracts like, so by feeling more motivated, productive and positive throughout the day you will naturally see more opportunities and moments to create positivity and abundance.

Rituals can be as long or as short as you please. No matter where you are in the world, what time commitment you have or your spiritual beliefs, the power of rituals is available to you at any moment. Maybe you want to sit down and create a really intentional ritual for yourself or maybe you only have a spare few minutes to ritualize and romanticize a small moment in your day. The rituals in this book have all been designed to feel manageable, keep you accountable and, most importantly, help to manifest your desires.

Living in a busy world full of distractions it can often be hard for us to find time to be truly intentional. Luckily, rituals are the quickest way to reconnect and focus on your desires. People often ask me why their desires aren't coming to fruition, and when I look into this with them, more often than not they are giving minimal or no energy at all to their desire while expecting their desire to be fully present and intentional with them. Remember, manifesting is like a divine mirror, and however you show up to the mirror of life is what is reflected back to you – it's a co-creation process, so if you're showing up with half-hearted energy, guess what you'll attract back? When we take the time to be fully intentional with our rituals, we create the space for our desire to be fully intentional with us – and when it comes to manifesting love, friendships, a house, money or career developments, this is what we want!

This book has been designed to guide and support you through your manifesting journey, whether that's an enquiry with your spiritual connection to the Universe, a journey of self-love and self-worth, or an improvement in your money mindset, career and purpose, health, alignment, limiting beliefs or relationships and love. Whatever it is, this oracle book has you covered.

How to Use
this Book

This oracle book is designed to give you quick and easy-to-follow guidance from the Universe. These messages from the Universe are expressed through affirmations and rituals, which you can connect with in two ways: either by seeking the answer to a burning question or by tuning in to what you need to know each day.

You might want to pick an affirmation in order to gain guidance on a specific situation, or perhaps you prefer to pick a ritual or mantra for the day each morning. Either way, these affirmations offer a simple and effective way of connecting to the Universe. Whether your concern is about romance, your career, health or even everyday decision-making, you can use this book to get clear answers and support from the Universe. The rituals work by using the law of attraction. Whether you pick one for yourself or another person, you will always attract the perfect affirmation as the message will match the question's vibration.

The book has been designed to work with and help you develop your intuition – remember, the answers are always within you. Whether you pick up this book as part of your daily manifestation ritual or just as and when you feel called to, there is no right or wrong. It's your ritual and your practice.

Using the book for the first time

The first time you use this book, take time to go through each affirmation in turn, connecting to the imagery and making sure you touch every page. This will infuse the pages with your energy, ensuring accurate rituals every time you use the book. Also, be sure to set the following intention while holding the book to your heart centre (in the middle of your chest):

Thank you, Universe, for clearing this book of any past energy and connecting it to my own divine energy. Thank you for delivering accurate affirmations and rituals for the highest good of all.

Each time you use the book, start by clearing it of any energy, as the book will easily pick up other people's energy if handled by them. You can do this by holding the book in your non-dominant hand and knocking the book with your dominant hand. This will knock out the energy and leave the book clear and ready for your questions.

Then, in your mind or out loud, ask your question to the Universe. An example would be:

'What can I do to manifest a pay rise?'

Or, you can set an intention, for example:

'Universe, what do I need to know right now?'

How to select an affirmation from the book

Begin flicking through the book, thinking of your question or intention as you go – I suggest doing this with your eyes closed if that feels good to you. When you receive an instinct or impulse to stop, trust this and pick a page with your finger. You can never pull a wrong affirmation, so follow the Universe. Once you have drawn one or more affirmations, take a look at them as they have the answer to your question or intention. Consider the words and illustration, noting any additional thoughts or feelings that come up, as these are messages from the Universe. Notice how you feel when looking at the affirmations, where your eyes fall on the page and if anything stands out.

Alternatively, if you don't want to pick an affirmation at random, you can also have a look at the contents page at the beginning of this book and see if you feel called to work with a certain affirmation or maybe to revisit one of your favourites. You can then turn to the corresponding page and work with your chosen affirmation without having to ask a question. Remember, this oracle book is your sacred connection with the Universe and your manifestations, so use it in a way that feels joyful for you.

While the book is designed to provide you with the perfect affirmation and ritual to embody the energy of each message, it is can also be a good idea to pick a few affirmations to try, as this strengthens the communication between yourself and the Universe. If you need more clarity, you can ask the Universe for a more detailed answer – simply close your eyes and start flicking through the book again until you feel called to stop.

If you receive a message that doesn't land with you or is not the answer you wanted, challenge yourself to dive deeper into it. It's easy to ignore a message and feel tempted to pick again, but sometimes the Universe delivers what we need rather than what we want. For instance, if you asked about improving your finances and then a message of self-love was picked even though you feel you have a good level of self-love already, challenge yourself to consider why the Universe would bring this message to you – maybe by working with self-love rituals you will unlock the door to financial abundance.

How to use the rituals

Each affirmation has a channelled explanation of its deeper meaning, related journaling prompts and rituals designed to help you embody the message. I have also included crystal recommendations to help you embody the energy of your affirmation, if they are available to you. You can use crystals to deepen your daily practice but they are not essential for effective manifesting.

Simply take the recommended rituals and tools and apply them to your question or intention. Practicing rituals regularly allows you to be intentional with your practice, to create consistency and to have fun with manifesting. A ritual is all about being present, so my hope is that this book allows you to come back home to yourself and to have lots fun along the way.

Take your time – you don't have to complete the rituals in one day, just make sure you take loving action towards them as and when you feel inspired to. The affirmations and rituals are designed to be positive, loving messages from the Universe. If you receive a message you weren't expecting, surrender and allow the Universe to deliver what is for your highest good.

How to store your book

Your book is personal to you, so feel free to place or display your book in a place that feels sacred to you. Personally, I like to keep my oracle decks and any books I'm working with either on my spiritual altar or in my bedside table so they are easily accessible.

If you'd like to create your own spiritual altar, this can be done using any special surface or location in your home. You may want to cleanse the space first using ethically sourced sage, incense sticks, crystals or an aura spray. Set your intentions for the space and think about what you'd really like to get out of working with your altar or the energy you'd like to co-create with your altar. You can then decorate your altar with anything that feels special to you, whether that be a crystal, feather, a candle, an ornament that has a special meaning for you or anything you feel called to place in this sacred space.

If you want to, you can keep this book on your altar or display the affirmation you pick for the day to remind you to check in with the ritual. There is no right or wrong with this, but I hope these suggestions can help you to set up a beautiful space in which to be intentional with your manifestations.

21 days to manifesting magic

It takes 21 days to change a habit, which means repetition is key when it comes to manifestation and embodying the energy of our affirmations. If you want to take these rituals even deeper, I suggest repeating an affirmation you feel drawn to for this period in order to really embody the energy and manifest the affirmation into your reality. Start by rating your belief of the affirmation on a scale of one to ten, one being 'I don't believe this to be true,' and ten being, 'I embody this and know it is true.' Write down where you start off on day one and document your progress through to day 21 – you will see how much your belief shifts!

You could also repeat your affirmations in the mirror. Known as 'mirror work', this is an incredible way to build your relationship with yourself, promote self-love and deepen your affirmation practice.

My intention is to help you unlock the power of manifestation through these powerful rituals so that you see love, abundance and magic enter your life. Please do let me know what manifests for you as a result of working with this oracle book and please do tag me online as I'd love to see what you pick!

Emma♡
xxx

@iamemmamumford | www.emmamumford.co.uk

IT'S
ALREADY
YOURS

The
Messages

ABUNDANCE POURS INTO MY LIFE EACH AND EVERY DAY

ABUNDANCE POURS iNTO MY LiFE EACH AND EVERY DAY

Abundance is our divine birthright. It surrounds us, and there are no limits to the amount of abundance we can receive. When we tune in to and appreciate the abundance that flows our way each and every day, even more manifests!

Today, the Universe is calling you to embrace this energy to manifest more abundance into your life. How can you step into the stream of abundance today?

Journaling prompts
- *What does abundance mean to me?*
- *What makes me feel truly abundant? (action this)*

Ritual
Over the next four weeks, keep track of all the abundance that comes into your life. Divide a page in your journal into four sections and give each a heading: Week 1, Week 2, Week 3, Week 4. Keep track of all the abundance and money that

comes to you each week and total it up at the end of the month. You can make this purely money-focused or add in any other abundance you receive throughout the month (such as signs, manifestations or wins). Either way, you'll be shocked at how abundant you truly are just from doing this exercise!

Crystal
Citrine – stone of abundance and manifestation.

AS I Do LESS, I ATTRACT MoRE ABUNDANCE To ME

It's easy to overcomplicate the manifestation process in the hope that if we do more, our desires will manifest quicker. But simply repeating the same practices might leave you stuck in the 'ask' step of the process.

Today, the Universe is encouraging you to slow down and take stock of where you need to let go and do less. By doing less, you create space for alignment and abundance to enter into your life.

Try this mantra this week and see what magic manifests into your life: '[your name] does less, [your name] attracts more'.

Journaling prompts
- *Where do I feel overwhelmed currently?*
- *What can I let go of now to do less and attract more?*

Ritual
Take a look at your manifestation practices and spiritual altar, and go through your journals. Declutter anything that's ready to

be released now. Look at your daily rituals and take note of anything that feels overwhelming or needs switching up. Consider changing any practice that feels a bit stagnant and simplify those that are too complex. It's not about the number of things you do each day, it's about how much joy is created and how you feel after doing your rituals – that's what really creates abundance in your life.

Crystal
Smoky quartz – for grounding and clearing negativity.

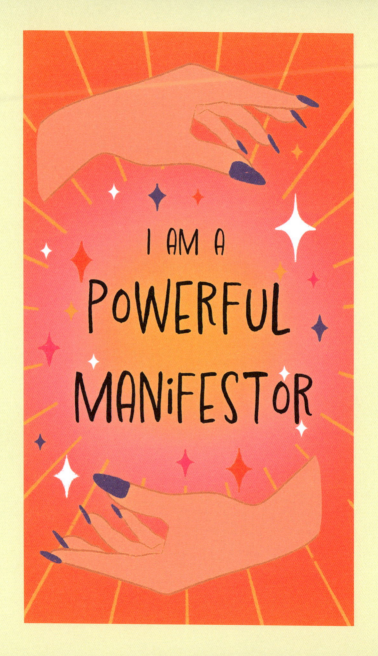

I AM A POWERFUL MANiFESTOR

Remember your power, Queen, and step into this now. Today, the Universe is reminding you of your innate power and your ability to manifest your dreams. Think back to all the wonderful manifestations that you have co-created and remember you are an active participant in the manifestation process. You have the power to bring this into your reality now.

Journaling prompts
- *How can I step into my power more?*
- *What are the qualities of a powerful manifestor?*
- *How can I embody these qualities?*

Ritual
Write down in your journal a list of all the things you've manifested this year or throughout your manifestation journey. Once you've finished your list, reflect back on it and express gratitude for every manifestation by saying, 'Thank you, thank you, thank you, Universe.' Think about how much joy each manifestation has brought into your life. Allow yourself to recognize that you are a powerful manifestor who has manifested incredible things.

Crystal
Tiger's eye – stone of confidence and personal power.

I AM STEPPiNG iNTo MY MoST ABUNDANT SEASoN YET

You are entering a new season in your life, one that requires your openness and willingness to expand into a new level of abundance and prosperity. As cyclical beings we are constantly ebbing and flowing through our own inner and outer seasons of life. Change is being ushered into your life now, which is exciting as change must always happen before your manifestation can be delivered.

Journaling prompts
- *What change do I feel needs to happen in my life?*
- *What changes am I feeling called to make right now?*

Ritual
To welcome in new energy or abundance you must purge any old or stagnant energy from your mind and home. So today or this week, when you can, make a commitment to declutter an aspect of your life – whether that be a room, your home, your work space, your mind or even your emotions. Get rid of

anything that is no longer serving you so that you can welcome in the bright and abundant season that awaits.

Crystal
Moonstone – stone of new beginnings, easing stress and strengthening inner peace.

I DON'T CHASE, I ATTRACT

Getting too attached to your desires can lead to disappointment with the law of attraction. This is why letting go is such an important step in the process. Today, the Universe is reminding you to become a magnet, to attract the energy of your desire and to become that version of yourself now, rather than chasing the idea of it.

Remember, the Universe is one gigantic mirror – so what are you showing up to the mirror with? Stop chasing and start preparing for the arrival of your manifestation!

Journaling prompts
Write down your desire, then imagine the future you having manifested this desire and answer the following questions:
- *What are you doing each day? How are you feeling? Who are you with? What are you wearing?*
- *What is one thing they're doing that you don't currently do?*

Ritual
Focus on how you can embody the version of yourself who has your desire by using the journaling prompts above. Close your eyes, centre yourself and tune in to the energy of the version of

yourself who has your manifestation. It may be easier for you to visualize yourself with your desire and see what that reveals. Embody and action these answers so that each day you are taking steps towards becoming this version of yourself.

Crystal
Blue kyanite – stone of chakra alignment, promoting balance and calm.

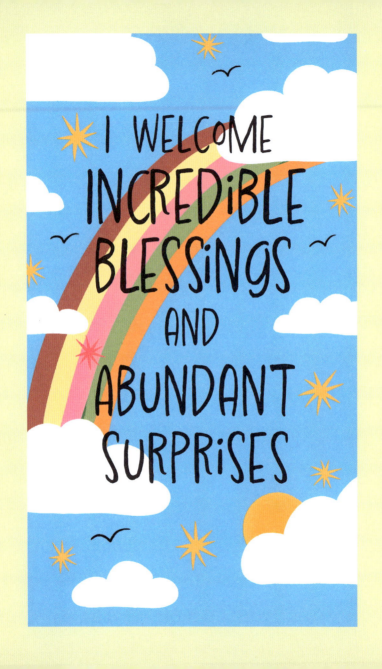

I WELCoME iNCREDiBLE BLESSiNgS AND ABUNDANT SURPRiSES

If you want to manifest true abundance into your life, you need to set regular intentions with the Universe. It's not enough to create a vision board and then expect to receive abundance weekly or even monthly! Vision boards are designed to be used long term, so having daily, weekly and monthly goals helps abundance to manifest regularly into your life.

Today, the Universe is reminding you simply to ask! If you need help or support – ask! If you want to manifest some abundance – ask!

Journaling prompts
- *What would I like to manifest today?*
- *How would I like to feel today?*
- *What would I like to experience today?*

Ritual
Use the journaling prompts to set an intention for the day ahead. List your desires in your journal in the morning and come back to them later on to see what manifested for you!

Then, get into the habit of setting daily, weekly and monthly intentions on each new moon or on the 1st of each month. I love to set three to five work goals, three to five personal goals and a money manifestation for the month.

By setting regular intentions, you will take steps towards your manifestation and see regular blessings and abundance!

Crystal

Jade – stone of abundance, luck and prosperity.

THE FUTURE I DESiRE
iS MANiFESTiNG NoW

Today, the Universe is telling you that your desires are close! Keep the faith and keep moving forwards. Remain open to all possibilities and know that you are worthy and deserving of all your heart's desires. It's time to switch into receiving mode and allow this abundance into your life now. Be sure to stay at your 50 per cent and allow the Universe to meet you halfway. Prepare for the arrival of your desire – the Universe is sharing with you that it's coming very soon!

Journaling prompts
- *Am I truly ready to receive my desire?*
- *How can I stay open to all possibilities and relax into receiving?*

Ritual
For today's ritual, you're going to prepare for your manifestation's arrival. Write a list in your journal of all the things you need to do before your desire arrives. What tasks need completing? Have you been putting anything off? Are there preparations to make? Whether it involves purchasing something, getting into shape, finishing a job or creating space for your desire to come in, write it down.

Remember, if you had nine months to prepare for a baby's arrival, you wouldn't wait until the day the baby was born to buy everything you need. So, prepare for your manifestation's arrival today and be sure to action your list moving forward. Get into the energy of receiving, Queen!

Crystal
Larimar – stone of peace, clarity, healing and outer manifestation.

WHAT I AM SEEKING IS SEEKING ME

Remember, Queen, your manifestations want you, too! Often, we can put so much attachment onto our desires that we feel the need to control or 'make it happen'. But you're not doing this alone. Today, the Universe wants to co-create with you and is inviting you to let go and let the Universe help. Become a magnet to your desire by embodying the energy of your desire and allow your manifestation to find you with ease.

Journaling prompts
- *How can I allow myself to trust in the Universe more?*
- *How can I let myself be met by my desire and the Universe?*

Ritual
Write a list of reasons why your manifestation wants you! For example: 'My dream home wants me because I'll really look after it and make it feel like a home.' Once you've finished writing your list, read your powerful reasons back to yourself and see how you feel. Remember, you are worthy of your desire, so focus on letting go of your attachment to your desire and co-creating with the Universe.

Crystal
Clear quartz – stone of clarity and intuition; an amplifier.

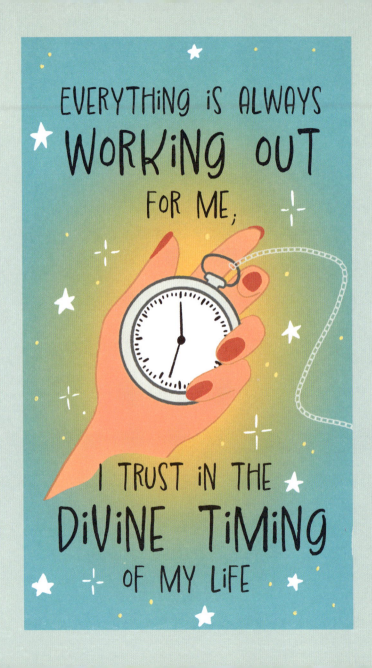

EVERYTHING iS ALWAYS WORKiNG OUT FOR ME; I TRUST iN THE DiViNE TiMiNG OF MY LiFE

Today, the Universe is reminding you to ground yourself to the present moment. There is a perfect 'divine' timing for everything in your life and now is the time to remember this. You are always exactly where you need to be, Queen, so celebrate the present moment and affirm that 'everything is always working out for me'.

If you constantly live in the future and think that you'll only be happy when your desire comes, you'll end up blocking the desire because you must be happy and enjoying life here and now. The present moment is a gift, too, and there is so much to be grateful for that is happening for you now. Your desire can only manifest in the present moment – so stay present and have fun! If you want to manifest love, for example, schedule time each week for date nights with yourself or friends.

Journaling prompts
- *How can I become more present today?*
- *What blessings or happy things are happening in my life currently?*

Ritual

Explore your relationship with divine timing and what it means to you. Take a page in your journal and write answers to the following questions: 'Where am I right now?' and 'What does divine timing mean to me?' Set aside time in the day to sit down and truly be present with this ritual. Explore your relationship with divine timing by writing a list of manifestations, big and small, that have come into your life and which you know, without doubt, happened at the right time for you. You could structure each one like this . . .

1. What I manifested: (a car, for example)
2. Did I feel truly ready to receive it?
3. If it had arrived any earlier, what would have happened?
4. What did I learn by embracing divine timing?
5. What was I doing right before it manifested?

Once you have a few examples to reflect on, you'll see how divine timing is never wrong and the Universe always knows the right timing for you. Return to this list whenever you feel attached to your desire.

Crystal

Sodalite – stone of insight, trust, clarity and intuition.

I ALLOW GRATITUDE TO FILL MY HEART AND FLOW INTO MY DAY

Gratitude is always the best attitude and can instantly transmute any negative energy. Today, the Universe is reminding you to invite gratitude into your heart and to allow it to enrich your day. It's very easy to focus on what's going wrong in life, but the Universe is telling you to look at the positives and count your blessings. There is always something to be grateful for!

Journaling prompts
- *What three things do I feel most grateful for right now?*
- *What am I grateful for about myself?*

Ritual
The ritual for today is going to really push you to feel the benefit and joy of a gratitude practice. Do a 'rampage of appreciation' list and challenge yourself to write 50 things you're grateful for. If you want to take your time and do this over a few days, that's fine. Once your list is complete, commit to a daily gratitude practice moving forward. Do this by writing down

I ALLOW

GRATITUDE TO
FILL MY
HEART

AND FLOW INTO MY DAY

three to five points of gratitude in your journal every morning. Word your sentences as: 'I am so grateful for . . . because . . .' and be sure to write down why! Writing down why takes this practice so much deeper and gives you all the juicy good vibes to set you up for manifesting success that day.

Crystal
Rose quartz – stone of unconditional love, compassion and appreciation.

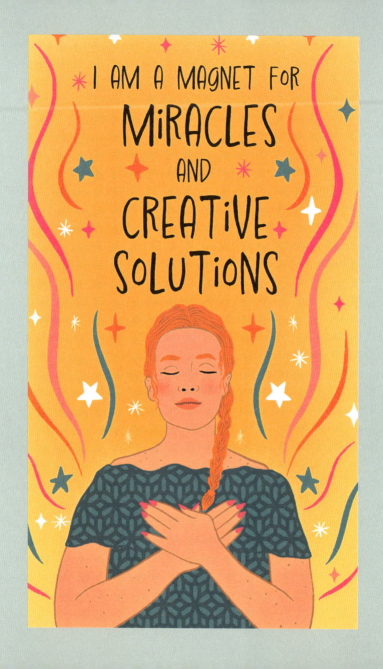

I AM A MAGNET FOR MIRACLES AND CREATIVE SOLUTIONS

Sometimes we hit a road block, where we feel as if we've tried everything but problems keep arising. It can lead us to a sense of helplessness. This is the Universe reminding us to step back, let go and let it take over – as the famous saying goes: 'Let go and let God'. Now is the time for you to step back and allow the Universe to assist. This will enable you to re-evaluate your situation and realign with the path in front of you. Be sure to listen to your intuition and allow creative solutions and miracles to enter into your day.

Journaling prompts

- *What situation in my life do I need a creative solution for?*
- *How can I let go today and let the Universe manifest miracles into my life?*

Ritual

Set an intention to invite creative solutions or miracles into your life. Perhaps you have a stressful situation and don't know how to handle it. Or maybe you feel that you have tried everything and are now blocked. You can set your intention with the Universe using the mantra below or you could create your own.

'Today, I let go of this situation and hand it over to the Universe. I invite divine support, miracles and creative solutions into my life to help me navigate this and feel at peace. I stand back now and allow these miracles and creative solutions to enter into my life. And so it is, thank you Universe.'

Once you've said the above mantra, challenge yourself to let go and let the Universe take over. Allow yourself to be supported in all ways and let miracles enter into your life.

Crystal
Carnelian – stone of creativity and motivation; an aid to the clearing of blocks.

I AM OPEN AND READY TO RECEIVE WHAT IS FOR MY HIGHEST GOOD

Often, we think we know better than the Universe when it comes to what is good for us. The truth is, the Universe can see everything and absolutely protects us from all things that are not for our highest good. When setting your intentions, therefore, it's really important to finish with, 'this or something better for the highest good of all'. Today, the Universe is telling you that there may be something you cannot quite see yet and to open up to receiving your desire in a way that's for the highest good. Let go of any expectations and allow the Universe to deliver in its own perfect way.

Journaling prompts
- *Do my desires feel aligned to me and my version of wealth?*
- *What could be my 'something better' if what I currently want isn't for my highest good?*

Ritual
For this ritual, you need to connect to the core energy of your desire to release any expectations. You can do this by using the meditation on the following page.

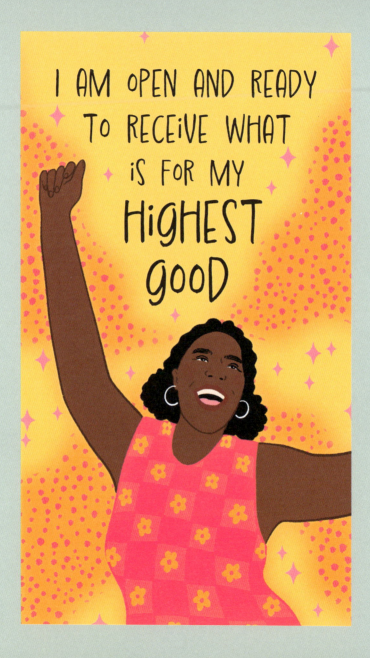

1. Close your eyes, centre yourself and take a deep breath in. On the exhale, let any stress or tension from your day be released from your body.
2. When you feel relaxed, focus on your manifestation with your eyes closed. See it play out in your mind's eye.
3. Now start to wipe away, physically with your arm or just in your mind's eye, anything that makes this desire tangible. So, wipe away any names, faces, places and so on, until you reach the core energy of your desire.
4. Notice how this energy appears to you – what colour is it? How does it make you feel? What words or feelings does this energy represent? Does it have any other characteristics, such as a noise or a smell?
5. Now open your arms and allow the energy to move closer to you in a way that feels right to this energy; don't force it. Notice how it feels as it gets closer to you.
6. Repeat this meditation as often as you feel the need.

Crystal
Pink opal – stone of releasing old patterns and attracting joy and love into your life.

I TAKE CARE OF MY ENERGY AND KEEP MY

MANIFESTATIONS SACRED

I TAKE CARE OF MY ENERGY AND KEEP MY MANiFESTATiONS SACRED

As we know, having too many cooks in the kitchen can not only cause stress, but also bring about varying results. The same goes with our manifestations. If lots of people know what you are manifesting, you can't guarantee all of them will support you. It is far better to keep your manifestations sacred, sharing them only with a trusted few until they are ready to be birthed into the world. Doing so will enable you to reclaim your power and protect your energy. This is the message the Universe has for you today.

Journaling prompts
- *How can I reclaim my power today?*
- *How can I take care of and protect my energy more?*

Ritual
Energy protection is a must for any Spiritual Queen. Today's ritual is to create a sacred group with two or three spiritual besties you fully trust. Use a social media messaging platform to post your gratitude, happy updates and support for one another, keeping them exclusive to this sacred group. Share

your manifestations. Name the group together, choosing something fun, and see what manifests for you all! Once your manifestations have arrived and it feels right, then you can share them with your wider group of friends and loved ones.

Crystal
Black obsidian – stone of protection and grounding; reflects negative energy back to its source.

I TRUST iN
THE DiViNE PLAN

'This or something better for the highest good' is a mantra to repeat whenever setting intentions with the Universe. While we may think we know what is best for us, sometimes the Universe must step in and help us see the bigger picture.

Today, the Universe is reminding you that you may not have the full perspective on a given situation. Trust that by stepping out of your own way you will create the space for something even bigger, better and more aligned to manifest.

Rejection, or a no, is only ever divine redirection to what is truly meant for you.

Journaling prompts
- *Do I believe the Universe is always working for my highest good? (If not, why?)*
- *When has the Universe showed up and supported me in the past?*

Ritual
In your journal, make a note of the times in your life when a rejection felt as if your manifestation or desire wasn't going to

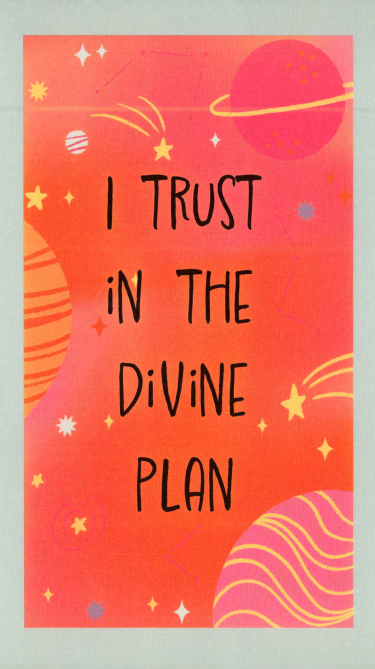

happen, but ended up bringing a positive result. This powerful exercise helps you to see divine redirection in action and how a 'no' will actually take you one step closer to a more aligned 'yes'. Remember, you don't want what's not meant for you!

Crystal

Amethyst – stone of intuition; releases anxiety.

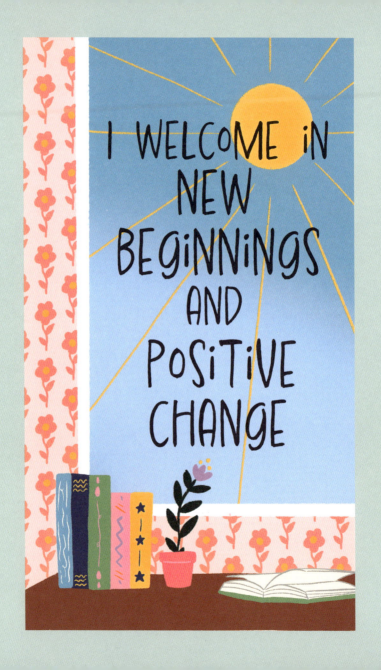

I WELCOME iN
NEW BEGiNNiNGS
AND PoSiTiVE CHANGE

Change is uncomfortable for all of us, but it is necessary for us to shift and evolve into our new reality. For our manifestations to come to fruition, we must first make a change – whether that's a habit, an energy shift or by creating space in our life. So, get ready for change in your life! The Universe is showing you with this affirmation and ritual that new beginnings are coming and they will bring in positive energy and blessings for you. Every great story starts with a new beginning and this is your time to welcome in a new chapter full of positivity, joy and abundance!

Journaling prompts
- *How do I feel about change and new beginnings?*
- *What can I do to ground myself during this transition?*

Ritual
This ritual invites you to try scripting to welcome in your new beginning with intention. Scripting is a great manifestation tool and really easy to do – all you need is your journal and a pen. Scripting is where you write a desire into existence using the present tense, as if it's already happened. For example: 'I am so

grateful for the smooth and easy transition into this new season of my life. I felt so supported and welcome in my brand new house!'

In your journal, write a letter to yourself or the Universe from your future self (the version of yourself who has already manifested your desire). Script your intentions for your future life in present tense and describe what this new season of your life is like. Think about what you'd like to feel and experience during this new beginning – what intentions can you set? What would you like to call in during this new beginning?

Once you're done, sign and date your letter (a year in the future, for example) and keep it safe in your journal. Reflect on it in a few months' time or at the end of the year, and see what manifested for you!

Crystal
Rainbow moonstone – stone of new beginnings, growth and divine inspiration.

MY iNTUiTioN KNoWS THE WAY AND iS ALWAYS gUIDING ME

Our intuition is our internal guidance, helping us navigate and never doing us wrong. Often, we ignore these nudges from the Universe, even though we know deep down what we need to do. Today, the Universe is reminding you to listen to your intuition and trust yourself more.

Don't just rely on external validation for decision making, take back your power and trust yourself. The way to build your intuition is through practice and by listening to your body and inner self when making decisions. Is it a hell YASS or a hell no?

Journaling prompts
- *When have I felt my intuition previously and was it right?*
- *What does my intuition feel or sound like to me (how can I tell it's my intuition speaking)?*

Ritual
This is a game called 'Hell YASS, Hell No'. When making a decision, big or small, take a moment to tune in and ask

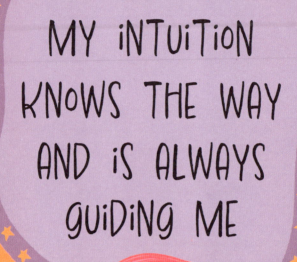

MY INTUITION
KNOWS THE WAY
AND IS ALWAYS
GUIDING ME

yourself 'Is this a hell YASS or a hell no?' Listen to yourself
and trust the first answer that comes to you. If it's not a hell
YASS, it's a hell no – trust that! If you're unsure, wait a couple
of days and ask the question again. You may be surprised, or
already know, that it was a hell no all along. Make all of your
decisions using this method and see how you feel afterwards
– does making these aligned choices bring you relief and joy?
Over time, if you practise this regularly, you will develop a
deeper connection with your intuition and be able to feel the
answers more clearly when making day-to-day and all-important
big decisions.

Crystal
Labradorite – stone of intuition, psychic ability and faith
in yourself.

THE UNIVERSE IS ALWAYS SUPPORTING ME

THE UNIVERSE IS
ALWAYS SUPPORTING ME

Trust, Queen. This is the time to trust in the unknown and allow the Universe to support you. It may feel as if you're taking a big leap of faith into the unknown right now, but your angel and spirit guide team want you to know they are here, supporting you every step of the way. You don't need to do this alone and the Universe wants you to know it has your back. Gently lean into this and know that you are always divinely guided and loved. Support is on its way and you're being invited to open your arms to receive this support now.

Journaling prompts
- *How can I support myself more today?*
- *What change or shift can I make today to help support me?*

Ritual
In your journal, make a list of those times in your life when the Universe has supported you. Perhaps a creative solution came into your life, or a person out of nowhere helped you out. Maybe money flowed to you unexpectedly when you were worried about your finances. We often forget the miracles that have already supported us in life, and in times of worry or stress

it can be hard just to 'trust'. Once you've written your list, reflect upon it and feel your belief in the Universe grow.

Crystal
Celestite – stone of angelic support; a calming influence on an overactive mind, worries and nerves.

I ATTRACT MONEY EASILY AND EFFORTLESSLY

'Money comes in, money goes out, money comes in, money goes out' was a mantra I adopted when working on my relationship with money. Just like the ocean, there is an unlimited supply of abundance in the Universe, yet we humans put energetic blocks on money and see it as limited. Get into the energy of receiving, and money will flow to you easily and effortlessly.

Journaling prompts
- *When has money flowed to me easily? (Write down any past examples)*
- *Do I trust that money will come back to me? If not, why?*

Ritual
Create a wealth bowl in your home, using crystals and a trinket dish that you feel really drawn to. For the crystals, I suggest green jade, citrine, pyrite, tiger's eye and emerald, or whatever crystals you'd like to use to attract abundance. Cleanse the crystals and bowl using aura spray, responsibly sourced white sage, local sage, palo santo, sunlight, moonlight or incense sticks.

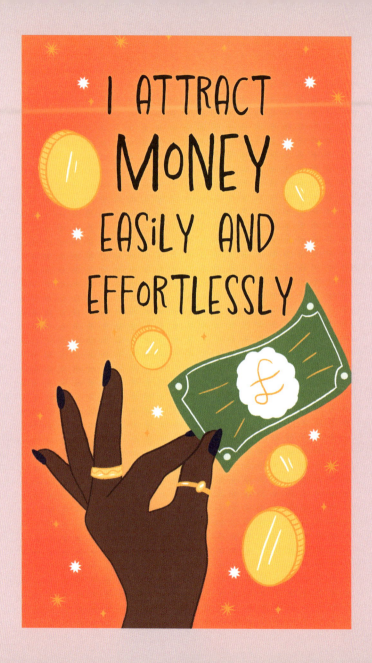

Set your intentions with the crystals and ask them to help you manifest money into your life for the highest good of all. Place the bowl on your desk, by your purse/wallet or in the far left corner of your house as this is traditionally the feng shui corner for wealth.

Crystal
Pyrite – stone of manifestation, money and wealth.

I FEEL POSITIVELY
WEALTHY WITH MY FINANCES

Having a positively wealthy mindset is more than just feeling good about money. It means embodying your personal version of wealth and financial goals, not someone else's.

Today, the Universe is reminding you to tune in to how you want to feel with money and what your own goals are with your finances. Make sure your goals feel good to you and consider how you interact with money, too. Set your sights as high as you feel called to and put your vision out there today.

Journaling prompts
- *What does wealth mean to me?*
- *When have I felt my most financially wealthy in life?*

Ritual
This is one of my favourite money mindset exercises and is really simple. Create a vision board that shows the Universe exactly how you'd like your relationship with money to be. Do this by writing words and drawing or sticking images on a piece of paper. Your financial reality vision board could reflect how

you'd like to feel with money in 12 months, or even in 5–10 years. The key is to be specific about what you'd like to feel or experience in terms of wealth in your life – be sure to include any business finances, too. Once complete, place your vision board somewhere you'll see it often.

Crystal
Garnet – stone of health, wealth and happiness; boosts energy and helps give you the passion to achieve your desires.

MONEY LOVES ME
AND I LOVE IT

In most relationships, it takes time and effort to get to know a person, and the same goes with money. Today, the Universe is asking you to look at your relationship with your finances and how you feel towards money. Do you feel in love with it? Invest time and energy in building this relationship up and watch your feelings towards your finances magically transform.

Journaling prompts
- *Do I feel I love money and does it love me?*
- *How can I build a loving relationship with money and get to know it better?*

Ritual
This is my 'money attraction game'! First, create a mantra related to manifesting money (such as the affirmation above). Repeat it three times in the morning, then go about your day.

The key to this game is not to focus on a given amount of money or where the money is coming from, but to be open to money and abundance pouring into your day from all sources.

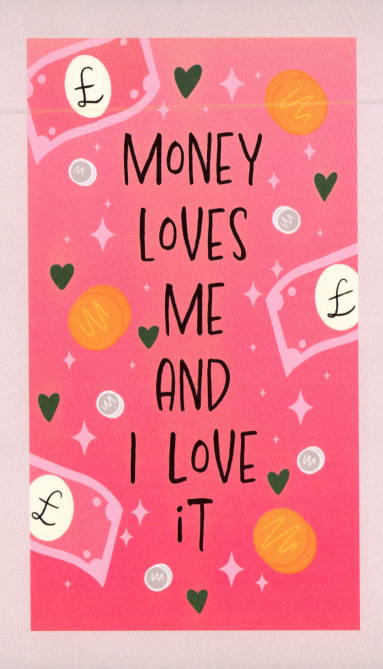

Throughout the day, be sure to write down when any money manifestations happen and say, 'Thank you, thank you, thank you, Universe, for the money that continues to flow my way.' At the end of the day, make a note of your total. Have fun, let go and really think about how you want to interact with money.

Crystal
Emerald – stone of money, luxury and wealth.

WEALTH AND
ABUNDANCE OF ALL KINDS
FLOW TO ME

Wealth is what you make it, Queen, it doesn't just have to mean money or finances. Abundance of all kinds flows to us each and every day and the Universe is reminding you of this. Tap into the vibration and energy of abundance and have some fun! Joy is the ultimate creator, so relax and enjoy being in the vortex of abundance. The more abundant you feel, the more abundance you will attract.

Journaling prompts
- *How abundant do I feel currently?*
- *Do I feel in the vortex and flow of abundance?*
  (If not, how can I get into the vortex and flow?)

Ritual
Focus on feeling in the vortex and flow of abundance with the Universe. Start off by making a list of things that make you feel truly abundant and wealthy. Remember, wealth is defined by

you – feeling wealthy doesn't just have to mean money and finances. Perhaps it's wearing a favourite jumper, doing a beauty ritual or walking past beautiful houses you aspire to own. Write your list down in your journal and aim to action one or two of the activities today! Spark those good vibes and feel as abundant as you can. This doesn't have to cost lots of money – it's all about what makes you feel abundant, and everyone will be different.

Crystal
Green aventurine – stone of wealth, prosperity, opportunity and optimism.

ALL OF MY RELATIONSHIPS REFLECT COMPASSION, LOVE AND JOY

Our relationships are divine assignments, here to teach us many lessons in this lifetime. It is through our relationships that we have the biggest opportunities to grow. But relationships can be testing.

Today, the Universe is encouraging you to express compassion. Love and harmony in your relationships must start with you and how you feel within yourself first and foremost, which will then be reflected in your outer experiences.

Journaling prompts
- *How can I invite in more self-compassion and compassion for others?*
- *Who and what am I grateful for in my relationships?*

Ritual
Write a list of statements about your loved ones in your journal. For example, 'I get frustrated that Jenny doesn't listen to me.' Sitting in front of a mirror, read each statement, then say three things that you're grateful for about that person, and why. For

example, your gratitude could be, 'However, I am really grateful for Jenny because she always makes me laugh.' As you shift each frustration into three moments of gratitude, your relationships will shift to focus on what joy these people bring into your life. Remember, though, that while gratitude is always the best attitude, your concerns and feelings are valid and should be taken seriously if you feel they need to be.

Crystal
Unakite – stone of patience, kindness and love.

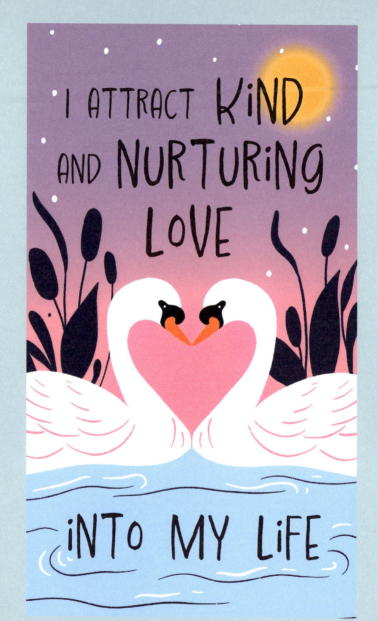

I ATTRACT KiND
AND NURTURiNG LoVE
iNTo MY LiFE

Love is coming your way, Queen! Whether you're already in a
relationship or it's your manifestation to be in one, the Universe
is affirming that love is all around you right now. Invite this kind
love in and allow it to transform your existing relationship, or
embody this energy to attract a new partner.

Journaling prompts
- *Do I feel I'm worthy of kind and nurturing love? (If not,
  why not?)*
- *How can I be kinder and more nurturing to myself?*

Ritual
Take a page in your journal and write the heading: 'My Dream
Relationship'. Below it, list down the characteristics, qualities
and traits you'd like that relationship to have. If you're in a
relationship already, list any changes you'd like to see. Dream
lists work every time, so make sure you're crystal clear on what
you'd like to experience. Keep your list safe and reflect back on
it when you meet someone or when you're next sorting through
your manifestations. Has anything manifested from your list?

Continue to check in with your list from time to time, to see if you want to level-up or clear previous intentions. We are always growing and evolving, so it always pays to refer back and see if anything needs to change – you can never do this exercise too many times!

Crystal
Pink tourmaline – a stone that helps to heal the heart from emotional wounds; infuses your aura with the energy of love and kindness.

I GIVE AND RECEIVE UNCONDITIONAL LOVE WITH EASE

At the end of the day, our spiritual journey always leads us back to unconditional love. Being in such a state allows you to experience ease, abundance, love and joy, so unconditional love should play a vital role in your manifesting rituals.

Today, the Universe is encouraging you to balance your heart chakra so that you can invite unconditional love in for yourself and others. Think about how you can manifest your desires from a space of unconditional love. When we love ourselves and others without conditions, we set ourselves free to experience so much wonder and joy.

Journaling prompts
- *Do I give and receive love in equal measure?*
- *What's my relationship like with giving and receiving love?*

Ritual
Think of ways in which you can give and receive more unconditional love in your life and plan to action something today to help you experience this.

You could also work with the colour green to balance your heart chakra (for example, wear green, eat green foods or take a bath with a green bath bomb).

Alternatively, find some balancing meditations online or work with a rose quartz crystal or with unconditional love affirmations like the one opposite. A powerful mantra for the heart chakra is the word 'yam'. Simply chanting this word will encourage its energy to balance your heart chakra.

Crystal
Rose quartz – stone of compassion and the giving and receiving of unconditional love.

I AM DEEPLY LOVED

BY THE UNIVERSE

I AM DEEPLY
LOVED BY THE UNiVERSE

The Universe wants you to know how loved you are, and at any moment you have a wealth of angels and spirit guides here to help and guide you. Call upon them now, as they are ready and willing to support and communicate with you through meditation, intuition, signs and synchronicities. Get to know your spirit guide team and invite them on your manifesting journey. Always know that in any moment, no matter how alone you may feel, you have a community of guides showering you with love and support.

Journaling prompts

- *When in my life have I felt deeply held and supported by the Universe?*
- *What have been my experiences with my spirit guide team so far?*

Ritual

Connect to your spirit guide team through the meditation on the following page and receive any words of wisdom or support they'd like to share with you.

1. Make sure you're comfortable. Take a deep breath in and, on the exhale, release all of the stress or tension from your day so far.
2. Centre yourself, and through your mind's eye, imagine a beautiful cave in a forest, and that you're sitting in this cave with a campfire in front of you and seats around you.
3. Next, set the intention to invite your spirit guide team into this space to join you. See them enter into this space now (don't force this, let them appear naturally).
4. Once everyone is seated around you, greet them in a way that feels right to you and let them introduce themselves to you and share their names.
5. Next, ask them if there is anything they want you to know right now that could help you manifest your desire? Listen to their responses.
6. Thank your spirit guides for their help and support, then come back into your body slowly and ground back in. When you're ready, you can open your eyes.

Crystal
Fluorite – stone of protection, grounding and clarity.

I AM ENOUGH

You are always enough, Queen. All too often, we feel as if we're not enough for something or someone. Your spirit guides are reminding you today that you always have been and always will be enough, and that it is your self-worth that needs attention and love right now. When you embody the knowing and feeling of being enough, your desires will magnetize to you.

Journaling prompts
- *Do I feel worthy and deserving of my desires here and now? (If not, why?)*
- *When in my life have I felt like I'm not enough, or too much?*

Ritual
Use mirror work to transform your relationship with yourself and your self-worth! Write 'I am enough' on a piece of paper and stick it on a mirror you see regularly. Each morning for the next 21 days, sit in front of the mirror with a hand placed on your heart and repeat this affirmation while looking into your own eyes. See how you feel as you repeat the affirmation and how that changes over the 21 days. You could also ask yourself,

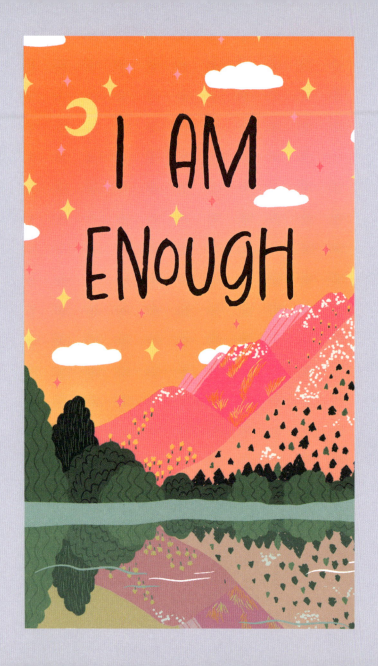

'What do I need today?' or 'What is the most loving thing I can do for myself today?' Be sure to honour any thoughts or feelings that arise. On day 21, see how your relationship with this feeling has transformed.

Crystal
Rhodochrosite – stone of self-worth; promotes unconditional love.

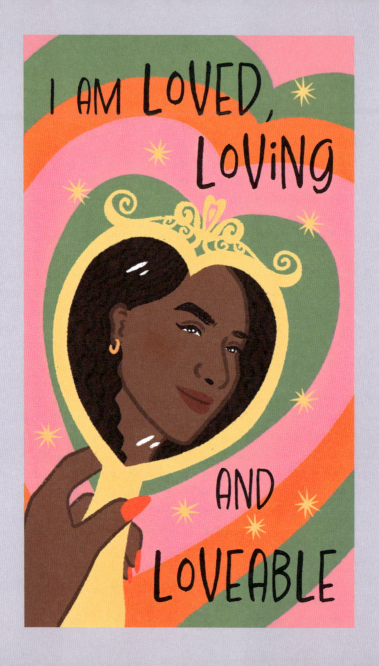

I AM LOVED, LOVING AND LOVEABLE

You truly are, Queen! Today, the Universe is reminding you that you are born worthy and deserving of unconditional love and support. The Universe is rooting for you and wants to remind you how loved you are. You make such a positive impact on so many lives. Your beautiful light is needed right now and your spirit team is encouraging you to shine!

Journaling prompts
- *What am I proud of myself for?*
- *What do I do each week to honour myself and fill my self-love cup?*

Ritual
Show yourself some love! In your journal, write down your proudest accomplishments. Besides the obvious ones, like becoming a mother or learning to drive, challenge yourself to go deeper. Include personal accomplishments, such as asking for help or overcoming a really difficult period. Once you're finished, keep the list safe and reflect upon it whenever you feel the need.

As a second part of the ritual, today you must do something to celebrate yourself and seal in this beautiful energy. Have a glass of your favourite drink, dance to some music, go out for a meal with friends or treat yourself to something. Do something physically to celebrate yourself today because you truly deserve it!

Crystal
Kunzite – stone of the heart, love and healing trauma.

I AM OVERFLOWING WITH ENERGY, LOVE AND JOY

When it comes to manifestation, joy is the ultimate creator in life, so tune in today and ask yourself where you need to spark more joy or energy?

The Universe is encouraging you to bring your energy and invite joy in to all you do today. Bringing big energy is key to making this happen for you now. Bring the energy, bring the love and bring the joy! You've got to meet the Universe halfway and this is what you're currently doing.

Journaling prompts

- *What brings me joy in my life?*
- *What activity or hobby makes me feel most alive and joyful?*

Ritual

Spark joy, energy and love in whatever way you feel called to and raise your vibes! Raising your vibration not only helps you to feel energized, happy and alive, it also helps in manifesting abundance to you. So, do something to help you achieve this,

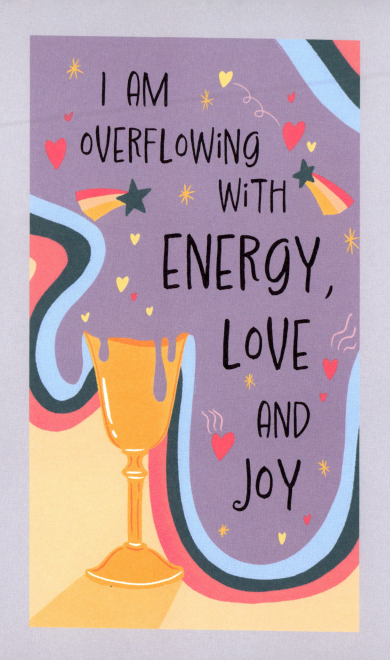

whether it's taking a walk in nature, trying yoga, having a dance party to your favourite high-vibe songs, working on your chakras or doing something for self-love. Raise your vibes and invite joy and energy in to all you do today.

Crystal
Dalmatian jasper – a stone that dispels negative thinking and brings energy and joy.

I AM WORTHY of **HAPPINESS,** **SUCCESS** AND **ABUNDANCE**

I AM WoRTHY
oF HAPPiNESS, SUCCESS
AND ABUNDANCE

Abundance can mean different things to different people and it's important that you know your core values and what happiness, success and abundance mean to you. Today, the Universe is reminding you that you are on your own path in life and however someone else achieves these things doesn't have to be the way you choose to do it. Your soul and intuition know the way, and the more you lean into this and trust yourself rather than listening to outside noise of what the path to success looks like, the quicker you will see shifts and abundance. You're the one living your life – no one else – so live it your way with your version of happiness, success and abundance.

Journaling prompts
- *What three wins, big or small, can I celebrate this week?*
- *What's making me happy and joyful at the moment?*

Ritual
Raise your vibes and bring joy into other people's lives with the 'pay it forward' challenge. Helping to create joy and happiness

in someone else's life is the perfect ritual for evoking joy. Today, do something kind for a stranger. Perhaps you could buy some flowers and gift them to someone, wrap a self-help book and leave it somewhere to be found or even donate your time to helping a good cause.

Whatever you choose to do, it doesn't always have to involve spending money. Think about ways in which you can bring a smile to a stranger's face and action them. See how bringing a smile to someone's face today helps your own mood, appreciation and happiness. If you like this ritual, be sure to make it a regular habit!

Crystal
Sunstone – stone of luck and good fortune.

I KNOW MY WORTH AND I STAND iN MY POWER

Standing in your power is a must for any Spiritual Queen. Voicing your needs and setting boundaries can sometimes feel scary, but it's time to stop saying yes when you really mean no.

Reclaim your power today by repeating 'I take back my power and call back all the lost pieces of myself.' How empowering does that alone feel? We give away our power both consciously and unconsciously every day. Repeating this affirmation frequently will help you to embody your self-worth and lovingly express it from a place of alignment.

Journaling prompts
- *Where in my life am I giving away my power?*
- *Do I lovingly express my boundaries and worth currently?*

Ritual
Time for one of my favourite self-worth rituals – it's time to get honest! This is all about lovingly voicing your needs to those around you and setting your boundaries. Take an honest look at your life and make a list in your journal of areas where you feel

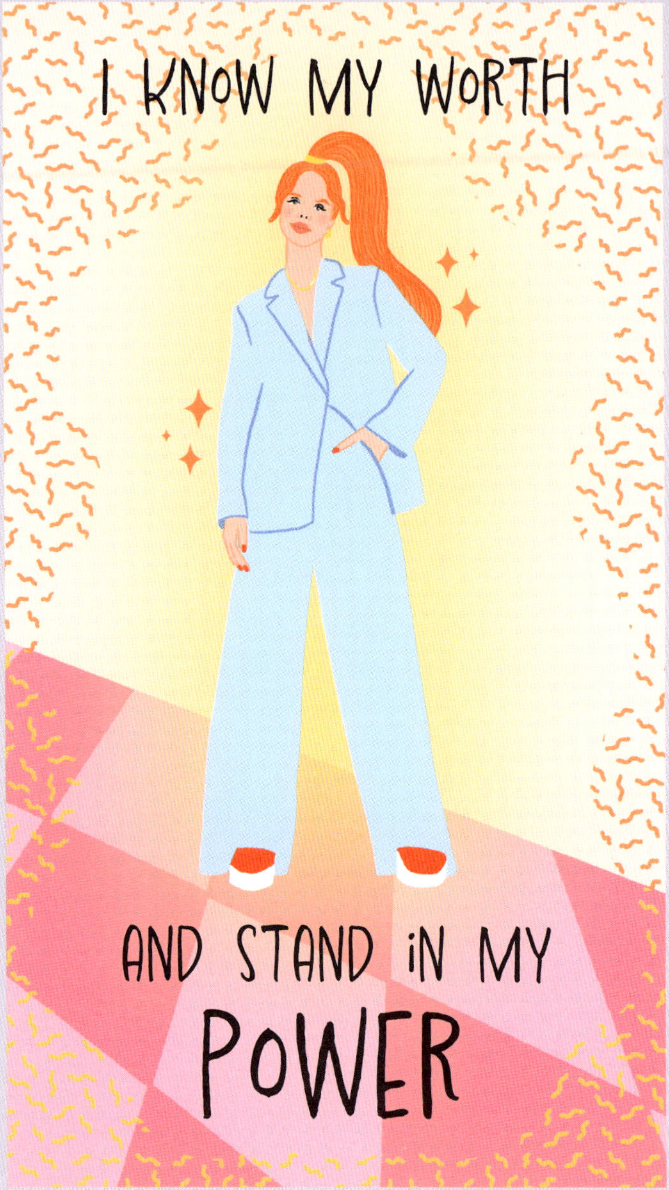
I KNOW MY WORTH
AND STAND iN MY
POWER

you need to lovingly set more boundaries or stop people-pleasing. Do you need to say no to going out with your friends so often, for example? Your practice moving forward is to action this list and gracefully implement these loving boundaries.

Voice your 'no' instead of saying yes to things you're not sure about and only say 'yes' when you truly mean it.

Crystal
Amazonite – stone of motivation, creativity and personal power.

I LoVE MYSELF
AND I AM PRoUD oF
WHo I AM

It's time to fearlessly love yourself, Queen. You deserve the
world and should be proud of all your hard work and dedication
to yourself and your desires. Often, we feel ashamed of old
versions of ourselves, feeling that we did something wrong or
weren't perfect. It's important to release any judgement and to
understand that you are always doing the best you can. Growth
and evolution are natural and that younger version of yourself
deserves love, too. Today, the Universe is inviting you to
express love and compassion to all the versions of yourself,
both past and present.

Journaling prompts

- *What am I proud of myself for?*
- *How can I celebrate myself more?*

Ritual

Acceptance and loving yourself unconditionally are part of a
process that takes time and patience. This affirmation and ritual
will help set you on the right path.

Self-love and acceptance list

1. Grab your journal and write two headings: 'Self-love' and 'Acceptance'.
2. Under the self-love heading, write down all the reasons why you love yourself. These must be true statements for here and now. It doesn't matter if there are 3 or 30 points.
3. Under the acceptance heading, write down what makes you proud of your past self. For example, 'I am proud of my past self for leaving a negative relationship.' List as many points as you can.
4. Once you have both lists, read each point out to yourself in the mirror while looking into your eyes. Notice how you feel as you read each point out loud. Once you're done, seal in this beautiful acceptance practice by saying: '[Your name], I really, really love you'.
5. If you like, you can repeat the 'I love you' statement for 21 days alongside this affirmation. Keep your lists safe and return to them anytime you want a self-love reminder.

Crystal
Red aventurine – stone of protection, love, independence and leadership.

I AM ALigNED WiTH MY PURPOSE AND CAREER

Alignment comes, firstly, from knowing and expressing your true authentic self and then, secondly, this is reflected into your outer experiences as you come into alignment with your desire. Today, the Universe is asking you to focus on alignment by concentrating on your purpose right now. If you don't feel in alignment with your purpose and career at the moment, this is your invitation to welcome alignment in to help you receive more abundance and joy from your work.

Journaling prompts
- *What does the word 'purpose' mean to me?*
- *Does my current job/career light me up and align with my purpose?*

Ritual
Today's ritual is a gratitude exercise for your career or current job. So often we focus on the negatives and what we are lacking, when we should be appreciating the blessings we have here and now. By focusing on the positives, you can transform your relationship with the work that you do and can actually

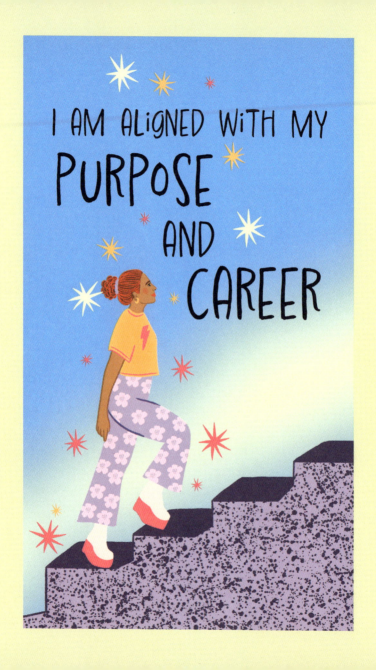

manifest the reality you do want. If you want to manifest something new, you must be present and appreciative with all you have.

In your journal, write down a list of all the things that you find frustrating in your current work and then flip these into gratitude. So, for example, 'It annoys me that I didn't get a pay rise this year,' might become 'I am so grateful I have a secure job that allows me to pay my bills on time each month.' Flip your current work stresses into blessings and see how this helps you to feel more positive towards your work, come into alignment and shift these situations to attract abundance.

Crystal
Moldavite – stone of soul transformation, purpose and alignment.

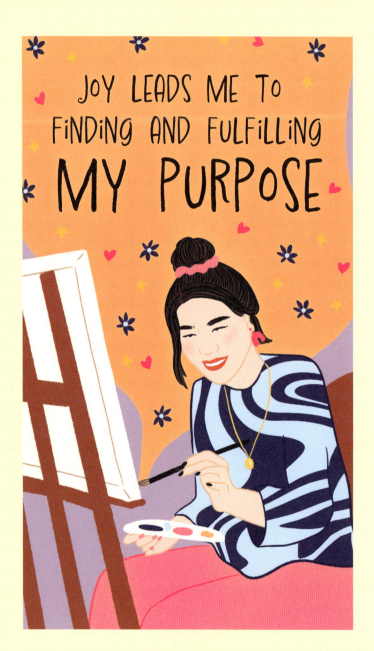

JOY LEADS ME TO FiNDiNG AND FULFiLLiNG MY PURPOSE

Finding our purpose is something we all want to achieve during our time on Earth. For some, that can feel like an impossible task. Purpose is something that can change with each new season of your life; what feels like your purpose now may not feel like your purpose in a year, and that's okay. This is a natural evolution and up-levelling that happens in life.

Right now, it's important to focus on what brings you joy and to follow your passions. Doing so will lead you to what you should be doing in this season of your life. So, wherever you are right now, know there is purpose to what you're doing in the world.

Journaling prompts
- *What is one thing I'd be gutted not to have done or created if I were to leave Earth tomorrow?*
- *What past jobs or careers have I really loved and why?*

Ritual
In your journal, write a list of past jobs that have brought you joy. Write a second list of your qualities, skills and strengths.

Close your eyes and relax. Now visualize all that you've written down and get into a place of feeling those joyful moments and emotions. Notice how you feel. Once you've visualized your lists, think about how the words relate to your purpose and what actions you can take to embody them more fully.

Crystal
Charoite – stone of inspiration, which helps identify higher meaning and your mission in life.

I AM FULL OF ENERGY AND GRATEFUL FOR MY BODY

Our bodies are miraculous, working hard to keep us alive and well each and every day! Today, the Universe is reminding you to be grateful for your wonderful body and to energize it with positive intentions and natural energy.

If you've been lacking energy recently, reflect on whether your habits and rituals are natural-energy boosters or depleting your sacred energy. Take steps towards creating a healthier routine and make time to really appreciate your incredible body and all it does for you.

Journaling prompts
- *Do I feel at home within my body?*
- *What gives me a natural energy boost? (What do I really enjoy doing?)*

Ritual
Make time for a mindful activity that makes you feel gratitude for your incredible body and all it does for you on a daily basis to keep you alive and well. Maybe that means writing a gratitude

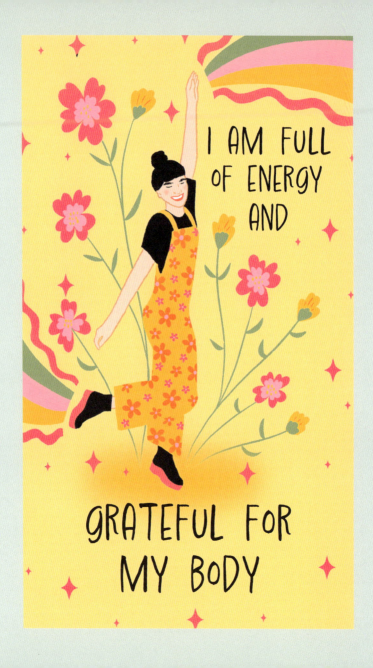

list for your health and body, or taking a mindful walk in nature, thinking about how your body moves and how it feels while walking. Perhaps you prefer mindful stretches or yoga or even some mindful dance. Tune in to whatever feels right for you and pick a mindful movement ritual to complete. Remember to stay mindful throughout, really tuning in to your body and how it feels during your chosen ritual.

Crystal
Blue apatite – stone of gratitude and manifestation.

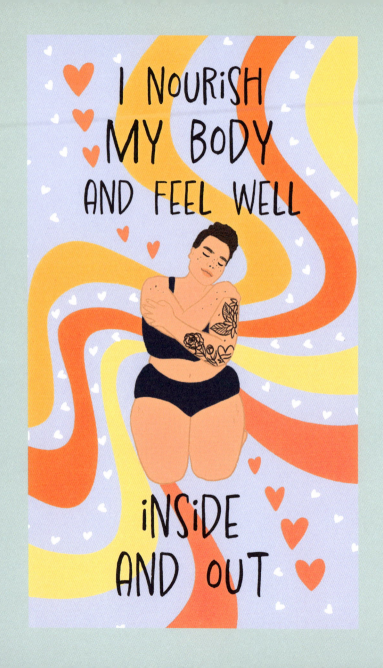

I Nourish My Body and Feel Well Inside and Out

Manifesting our desires and coming into alignment involve mind, body and spirit, yet we often forget about the body. When we nourish our bodies, we regulate the nervous system and feel so much better within ourselves.

Today, the Universe is inviting you to tune in to your body to discover what it needs right now. Your body is calling out for balance and nourishment, so go within and listen to what it has to share with you today.

Journaling prompts
- *What is one thing I do currently that I know isn't supporting my body's nourishment?*
- *What are my favourite nourishing meals or practices?*

Ritual
Create a mindful meal to nourish your body. Tune in to whatever your body is craving and turn both the preparation and eating of it into a ritual. Maybe bless the ingredients or express some gratitude while cooking. Set the scene at the table by lighting a

candle or playing relaxing music. Take a moment before eating to breathe in the aroma and really look at the different colours and textures of your meal. As you eat, take time to chew your food mindfully. Really savour the flavours and feel the nourishing effects of the food on your body.

Crystal
Agate – stone of nourishment that is also grounding.

MY BODY iS HAPPY, HEALTHY AND THRiViNG

When practicing self-care, we often focus on the cognitive and spiritual side of self-care and forget our beautiful body! To nurture a happy, healthy and thriving body, you need to be mindful each week of what you're doing for self-care and what you're putting into your body to support it. Whether that's with fitness, vitamins or even honouring your body's needs, it's important you listen to your body. This is the case for your whole body, inside and out. It's time to pamper your body and worship the skin you're in.

Journaling prompts
- *What do I do on a weekly basis to pamper my body?*
- *How can I look after my body and skin and ensure that they are thriving?*

Ritual
Self-care is a weekly must for any Spiritual Queen. Treat yourself by giving your wonderful body a pamper session, whether that's a nice body scrub and moisturizing treatment or a nourishing facemask and serum. See what you feel called

to do and celebrate your beautiful skin and body. Set the scene for your pamper session with some music, maybe a glass of your favourite drink and even some sweet treats. Dedicate some time to you today and celebrate the skin you're in!

Crystal
Amber – stone for emotional balance and lifting your spirits; purifies the aura.

I AM AT PEACE
WITH MY INNER CHILD
AND INNER WORLD

Within us all is a small, childlike version of ourselves: our inner child. They are part of our subconscious and remain with us throughout our entire life. This version of you is communicating with you today and wants to be reassured and loved.

Spend some time connecting with your inner child and strengthening your relationship. Just because we grow up, it doesn't mean we have to lose the childlike magic and awe in our lives. Invite that joy back into your life to create peace between you and your inner child.

Journaling prompts
- *How is my inner child feeling and what do they need from me right now?*
- *What does my inner child want to do for fun this week?*

Ritual
Today's ritual is to invite fun and childlike magic into your day. Start by placing a hand on your heart space and close your eyes. Invite your inner child into your heart space (you may feel,

hear, see or just sense that they are there). Once aware of their presence, give them a big hug, tell them you love them and ask them the above prompts. Write down your answers to these questions and make a commitment to action them this week.

Crystal
Mookaite – stone of healing inherited patterns, ancestral trauma and lineage.

I AM PRESENT, GROUNDED AND AT PEACE

Mother Earth is calling you to get rooted and ground yourself in the present moment. The only time you can receive your manifestation is in the present moment so, today, challenge yourself to become present. Put your technology away, get out in nature and connect back with your breath, your body and the Earth. Immersing yourself in nature can be so therapeutic for the mind, body and spirit. As you ground into the present moment, allow waves of peace to wash over you.

Journaling prompts
- *What can I do today to ground myself?*
- *What task or exercise can I choose to be truly present with today?*
- *How do I plan to achieve this?*

Ritual
Today's ritual is all about grounding, Queen! Try the visualization on the following page to become truly grounded and present.

1. Make sure you're comfortable, with feet rooted on the floor. Close your eyes and take a deep, cleansing breath in. On the exhale, let go of any stress or tension from your day.
2. Still with your eyes closed, visualize a bright white golden light just above the top of your head. See it start to pour down like a liquid or light and move through your entire body from your crown to the tips of your toes.
3. Once this white golden light has travelled all the way down your body, envisage brown and red roots (like tree roots) emerging from the soles of your feet. Picture them growing and burrowing down through the floor of the building you're in and into the Earth.
4. See these roots moving down further and further down until they reach the core of the Earth. In the core of the Earth, see a smoky quartz crystal. See your roots wrapping around this crystal, grounding you in.
5. Notice how you feel with your roots anchored and a sense of feeling safe and held. When you're ready, you can open your eyes. Return to this visualization any time you feel the need to ground back in.

Crystal
Lithium quartz – a stone that uplifts, balances and soothes.

I RELEASE AND LET go of THE PAST WiTH EASE

The past is behind us, the future never comes and all we have is the present. Yet so many of us rob ourselves of the gifts and blessings the present moment can bring. Queen, it's time to release the weight you've been carrying and let it go. Today, the Universe is lovingly reminding you that your desires and dreams need you to be here in the present moment. It's safe to let the past go now and move towards radical acceptance and love for yourself and others. Allow acceptance to wash over you and find peace with what was and what is here and now.

Journaling prompts
- *Where in my life do I feel stuck in the past and can't let go?*
- *What does holding onto the past give me?*

Ritual
This ritual explores how items and the energy of our surroundings can also impact what we're energetically holding onto from the past. Today, clear out anything from your past that is no longer serving you – whether that's an ex's sweater, photos or even an item you were gifted that no longer feels in

alignment. You don't have to get rid of everything associated with your past, but hold the item and see how it feels to you.

It may also be helpful to cleanse your home or the spaces that you've been storing these items in. You can cleanse your home or space using aura spray, white sage (try to get locally sourced sage if you can), palo santo or incense sticks. Clear away any past or negative energy from these items, then release (get rid of) them or pass them onto a new loving home if you can.

Crystal

Rutilated quartz – stone of letting go of the past; promotes forgiveness in all areas of your life.

I RELEASE
ANY BLOCKS THAT
HOLD ME BACK

Lack of belief and fear of what might (or might not) happen are top reasons for manifestations becoming blocked. Today, the Universe is highlighting this for you, encouraging you to reflect on any blocks you have and to release them for good. Every single human being has limiting beliefs and fears formed from their earlier years and experiences in life and these then form patterns and deeply ingrained beliefs about ourselves and life. When you clear the way of resistance you create the path for abundance to flow to you.

Journaling prompts
- *What stops me from receiving my desires currently?*
- *What beliefs or fears do I think are blocking me?*

Ritual
The 'letting go' ceremony on the following page will help you to release any blocks that may be coming to the surface. Performing the ritual on a full moon will enhance its effects.

I RELEASE ANY
BLOCKS THAT
HOLD ME BACK

Take a fresh page in your journal and write answers to the following questions:

1. What does my inner critic/ego want me to know right now?
2. How has this been blocking my manifestations?
3. When did I first start feeling this way or having this trigger?
4. Am I ready to release this now?
5. What has this block taught me?

Sign and date your journaling to confirm that you're ready to release it. Tear the page from your journal and burn or destroy it in a safe manner. When burning or destroying your page, you could repeat a mantra, such as, 'I now fully release and let go of this block. I am ready to let this go and embody a new positive belief that brings me into alignment with my desire. And so it is.'

Crystal
Black tourmaline – stone of protection from negative emotions and intentions; clears the aura and promotes balance.

I RELEASE ATTACHMENT AND LET GO OF THE OUTCOME

An important step in the manifesting process is to surrender your desire and release any attachment to it. This is absolutely one of the hardest parts of manifesting, but it is essential to your success. Don't worry, though, this does not mean giving up on your vision. Today, the Universe is encouraging you to surrender your expectations to the divine and to allow the Universe to bring this into your life in the most perfect way. Releasing your attachment and expectations will create the space for your desire to come to fruition.

Journaling prompts
- *What are my expectations around my desire?*
- *Why do I feel like I need my desire so soon?*

Ritual
Letting go and surrendering is a natural process that can't be forced, so ease into today's ritual with a gentle surrendering practice. Remember, needing nothing attracts everything! Writing in your journal, explore any fears you have of your desire not happening and your reasons for gripping on so tightly to its outcome. Ask yourself the questions on the following page.

- *What's the worst thing that would happen if my desire didn't manifest?*
- *What is lacking in my life currently that is making me so attached to this desire?*
- *What do I think this desire will give me?*
- *How can I give this to myself here and now?*
- *What season of my life am I in right now and how can I enjoy the view?*
- *What are three positive things I can do here and now that I may not be able to do when my desire comes?*

Crystal

Dioptase – stone of letting go and emotional freedom.

I AM BALANCED
AND iN AliGNMENT
WiTH MY HiGHER SELF

Your higher self is the most evolved version of you – free of limiting beliefs and fears or blocks that you've come to embody in this lifetime. Today, the Universe is encouraging you to connect to your higher self as the being that holds the answers to your question. Your higher self is always there to lovingly guide you. It wants to connect with you, to help you achieve whatever it is you seek. You can connect to your higher self through journaling, meditation and by intention.

Journaling prompts
- *How can I bring balance into my mind and life?*
- *Who is my higher self? (describe them)*

Ritual
Follow these steps to connect to your higher self:

1. Make sure you're comfortable. When you're ready, close your eyes and take a deep breath in. On the exhale, release any tension or stress from your day so far.

2. Still with your eyes closed, picture your higher self in your mind's eye. Visualize being in a scene in the future. Take note of what the scene is and what your higher self is doing.
3. Walk over to your higher self and greet them in a way that feels right to you. Ask them: 'What is it you want me to know right now?' Listen to their response.
4. Be open to any pearls of wisdom or advice that your higher self wants to share with you today and thank them for their guidance and support.
5. When you're ready, come slowly back into your body and allow yourself to ground back in, feeling lighter, brighter and full of positive energy. When you're ready, you can open your eyes.
6. Write down anything your higher self shared with you and make it a regular ritual to connect with your higher self when you need support or guidance.

Crystal
Apophyllite – stone of spiritual growth, intuition and cleansing.

I RADiATE PoSiTiVE ViBES AND ENERGY

Today, the Universe is encouraging you to have fun and spark joy! If you'd like to manifest positive vibes and the feeling of being in alignment, then work on cultivating habits and a routine that fills your day with fun and joy. Remember, joy is the ultimate creator, so the more fun you're having, the more positive energy you'll create in your life. Express your true self today and put yourself first!

Journaling prompts
- *When do I feel my most positive and joyful? (Action these regularly if you don't already)*
- *What does alignment mean to me?*

Ritual
Today's ritual is about having fun and manifesting alignment! In your journal, write down the following heading: 'What Does Fun Mean to Me?' Below it, write 25–30 points. Your first 15 points may be obvious things that you do often, such as dancing or baking. For the next 15 points, you'll really be challenged to dive deep into what fun actually means to you and you may

even discover some things you haven't done for a long time. Go deep with this exercise today and then action one of these points each week. Make time for fun and for being in the present moment!

Crystal
Calcite – stone of positivity, serenity and spiritual growth.

LiFE iS EASY,
CALM AND PEACEFUL

Life brings us many different seasons, whether of peace and happiness or of emotional and physical hardship. Life ebbs and flows in a cyclical way, so remember in more challenging times that 'this too shall pass'.

Today, the Universe is reminding you that you can invite peace into a tricky situation — all you need to do is ask. Remain grounded in your truth, prioritize your self-care and let the Universe hold and support you.

Journaling prompts
- *What doesn't feel easy or calm in my life currently?*
- *How can I create more ease and flow in my day-to-day life?*

Ritual
Reflect upon your answers to the above journaling prompts and try to remove any heaviness from your life where you can. Focus on prioritizing your peace and creating ease within

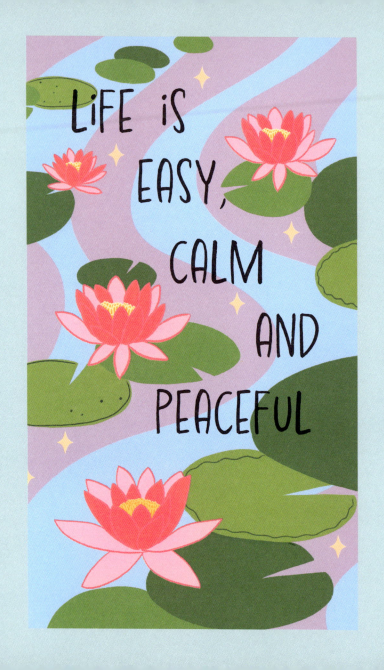

yourself today. How can you bring more ease and flow into your day? Be sure to choose practices and activities that feel light and joyful to you. You may feel called to declutter your home, workplace or even your emotions. Let go now and create the space for ease and flow to manifest.

Crystal
Malachite – a stone of balance that uplifts and helps create ease.

About the Creators

Emma Mumford is the UK's leading law of attraction expert. She is an award-winning life coach, law of attraction YouTuber, bestselling author, speaker and podcast host of the the number one spirituality podcast on iTunes, 'Spiritual Queen's Badass Podcast'. **www.emmamumford.co.uk | @iamemmamumford**

Emmy Lupin is an illustrator who is inspired by looking at life through a female lens. Her artwork is playful, relatable and empowering, with a bold use of pattern and colour and a decorative, hand-drawn style. **www.emmylupin.com. | @emmylupinstudio**

Author acknowledgements

Thank you to the wonderful team at Quercus for believing in me and my work. Thank you to Emily, my commissioning editor, for making this possible, to Emmy, the illustrator, for bringing such wonderful energy into this project, and to the designer, Tokiko, for helping to bring this vision to life. A big thank you to my loved ones, friends and family for your unconditional support and love towards me and my work. I couldn't do any of this without you and every day you show me how magical manifestation can be, simply by being in my life. Finally, to all of you, my loyal and lovely community: thank you for being the best community a Spiritual Queen could ask for and for supporting my work. Because of you, I get to create these beautiful things and I am so lucky to have you all in my life. Thank you, thank you, thank you, Universe x

First published in Great Britain in 2024 by
Greenfinch
An imprint of Quercus Editions Ltd
Carmelite House
50 Victoria Embankment
London EC4Y 0DZ

An Hachette UK company

A CIP catalogue record for this book is available from the British Library

HB ISBN 978-1-52943-592-4
eBook ISBN 978-1-52943-593-1

10 9 8 7 6 5 4 3 2 1

Cover and interior artworks by Emmy Lupin Studio
Designed by Tokiko Morishima and Ginny Zeal

Printed and bound in China by C&C Offset Printing Co., Ltd.

Papers used by Greenfinch are from well-managed forests and other responsible sources.